Make It Modern
MACRAMÉ

The Boho-Chic Guide to Making Rainbow Wraps,
Knotted Feathers, Woven Coasters & More

stash BOOKS.

an imprint of C&T Publishing

Make It Modern
MACRAMÉ

The Boho-Chic Guide to Making Rainbow Wraps,
Knotted Feathers, Woven Coasters & More

MIA BOYLE
Peanut Butter & Jelly Bean

Text and artwork © 2021 by Carmea (Mia) Boyle

Photography © 2021 by C&T Publishing, Inc.

Publisher: Amy Barrett-Daffin
Creative Director: Gailen Runge
Developer: Peg Couch & Co.
Editor: Katie Weeber
Cover/Book Designer: Michael Douglas
Production Coordinator: Zinnia Heinzmann
Photography by Carmea (Mia) Boyle

Published by Stash Books, an imprint of C&T Publishing, Inc., P.O. Box 1456, Lafayette, CA 94549

Library of Congress Control Number: 2020949726

Printed in the USA

10 9 8 7 6 5 4 3 2 1

To my children, who are my constant source
of inspiration, joy, and creativity.

Contents

27

37

51

64

96

69

102

83

108

INTRODUCTION

After earning a university degree and working for ten years in the scientific field, I was blessed with identical twin girls. This impacted my life in the most unexpectedly beautiful way. Spending a lot more time at home opened the door for me to explore my creative artistic passion. I started to sew for the girls (buying two sets of brand-new *everything* was expensive!), making them bibs (reflux babies), bows, and blankies. When I started to make for other people, my online shop and Instagram page was born—Peanut Butter & Jelly Bean.

After a few years and another baby (a beautiful little boy), I discovered macramé and fiber art. It became a form of meditation and relaxation for me (three kids less than three years old is wild!). I absorbed inspiration from online sources and social media and taught myself all the basics. My art gained a fan base very quickly, and I was making and sending it worldwide.

I feel incredibly lucky and honored that my customers and clients let me create art for the most sacred places in their homes—nurseries, bedrooms, offices, and family rooms. I honestly put a little bit of love into every piece I create and feel such pride when I see them hanging in their forever homes.

Many people are inspired by my art for their own creations, which I embrace with open arms. This creative journey has brought me so much fun, freedom, and relaxation that I find it a great privilege to guide and empower anyone else on the same path.

And that's exactly what this book is all about. I've included all of my most popular pieces of work—the art I get asked about daily. I wanted to offer instructions outlining my way of doing things and provide the potential to inspire you to put your own spin on your works of art.

The beauty of macramé and fiber art is that the techniques and possibilities are endless. The combination of knots, fibers, and patterns can be used in so many ways. This book starts at a beginner level and works through increasing levels of difficulty. I have included a limited number of knotting techniques to avoid overwhelming the process and to demonstrate that just a few knots can create a variety of projects. Please keep in mind that my way is not the only way, and it is important to find your own groove—and let your imagination run wild!

Meet the Author

Where are you from?

I grew up in a little country town in Tasmania (a small island state off the south coast of Australia). A lot of my family still live there, and I visit frequently—it is beautiful! Now, I live in Queensland, Australia, in a small coastal suburb of Northern Brisbane.

How did you get started in macramé?

I always wanted to learn! One day when my babies were napping, I had a few spare hours, so I taught myself some simple knots following YouTube videos, and it all grew from there.

What do you love about the craft?

The texture, shapes, patterns, and symmetry that can be created with fiber art. I find the action/knotting therapeutic, and the results are really beautiful to look at and touch.

Do you find knotting relaxing?

Yes! I love to just string up some cotton and start knotting without a pattern and see where it takes me. It gives me some time to shut off my mind and just go with the flow of creativity. Just standing/sitting in one spot with nowhere else to be—I think we all need that sometimes.

Can you tell us about your studio (or where you make your items)?

My whole house is my studio—there is artwork dripping off almost every wall! But I have a small nook off my living room that is my design space—it is really brightly lit and is right next to my coffee machine! Consequently, it is my favorite place to be. My kids love to sit there with me and draw and color while I'm working, too. But I dream about having a huge studio space with supplies to paint, knit, crochet, sculpt, woodwork, metalwork, build, macramé—any art or craft my heart desires. It would be heaven!

What inspires your art?

Nature. I love patterns that you can see in leaves, grass, feathers, trees. I love the texture you can see in the ocean, clouds, and stones. Also, interesting artwork that makes your eyes smile and your hands want to feel.

What does boho mean to you, and how does that influence come out in your art?

Boho style, to me, screams layers, textures, patterns, earthy colors, and neutrals. It can sometimes mean breaking all the classic style rules and mixing things that shouldn't work together, but they do. It draws inspiration from elements in nature.

We absolutely love your design style... can you tell us how you landed on it?

My style has definitely been an evolution. I have always loved the boho style, but initially, I only wanted to work with neutral colors (think natural linen, creams, light grays). I was horrified when a client asked me to use some color! After a little research, it only took me about an hour to fall in love with the rich earthy tones of cinnamon, rust, mustard, sage, blush, etc. I still only work with quite a modest palette, but I suppose it has become my signature.

The color combinations that can be achieved with just a few beautiful tones is astounding. I don't know what, if anything, makes me any different from anyone else creating the same style of art. Still, I have an eye for detail that can be quite annoying at times. Things have to look "just right" before I put my name to it. Really, I just make things that I want to hang on my own wall. And it turns out, sometimes other people would like to hang those things on their walls, too!

You have an online shop, a very popular Instagram feed, and three little ones at home! How do you manage it all?

Haha! Sometimes I don't! I can juggle, but sometimes balls get dropped—and that's ok. I have learned to loosen my expectations and just allow things to unfold. You have to know which balls can be dropped and which ones can't. I know what my priorities are, and I am very lucky to have a life that supports them.

What do you hope readers get out of this book?

The main thing that I hope this book provides is inspiration! I hope it guides people to create some of my favorite projects as a starting point, but then I hope the reader/maker can go on to discover his or her own unique style.

What's your favorite music to listen to while creating?

Anything acoustic, indie, or folk. I also love classical (nerd alert) and rock (I'm an 80s child!).

Mia Boyle is an innovative fiber artist from Brisbane, Australia, and the founder of *Peanut Butter & Jelly Bean by Mia* design studio. Her distinct designs have garnered more than 80,000 followers on Instagram, and she holds a consistent five-star rating on Etsy, where she has been selling her work since 2016. In addition to being a busy entrepreneur, Mia is a devoted mom of three children and a compassionate crafter who donates five percent of monthly profits to charity. Follow Mia's creative journey at @pbutterandjbean.

Getting Started

Let's get to it! With a few strands of cotton and some basic knots,
you can create a whole collection of macramé projects for your home.
In this section, we will review all of the tools and materials you will need
for the projects in this book and tutorials for making each knot.
Once you have read this chapter, you will be fully equipped
to tackle any project you would like.

Tools & Materials

Before starting any of the projects, it is important to get all the items you need organized. Each project includes a list of the specific tools and materials required to make it. When I first started macramé, I literally had a roll of cotton and some cheap scissors, so you really don't need much and will work it out as you go. But to make it easier, let me outline everything you need to make all of the projects in this book so you are prepared.

Good sharp scissors. Investing in some high-quality scissors will change your (fiber art) life!

Macramé cotton. There are so many different types of cotton string to use, and each one will make your projects turn out a bit differently. For the projects in the book, I used either 3mm or 5mm soft, single-twist, premium macramé cotton. Find a great cotton supplier in your area and ask for their opinion. Experiment with several different varieties until you find one that you prefer.

Tape measure. Most of the time, I don't measure my cotton and just estimate how much I will need, but that comes with practice and experience. I have measured all of the projects in this book so you have specific lengths to guide you while you are learning.

Clear-drying fabric glue. I use this a lot in my work. I find it gives a neater finish in many cases than stitching. It also works well to secure loose ends.

Yarn. All the yarn that I use is selected purely for its color. It can be wool, acrylic, or a blend, thin or thick—it will all work. And the variety actually adds a bit of interest!

Other fiber and additions. You can use other fibers and materials to embellish your work. Crystals, wooden or metal beads, silk, raffia, scrap material, shells, etc. all look great. Swivel clasps, earring hooks, and jump rings are also used in this book.

Hairspray or spray starch. I personally don't use spray starch, but it can be sprayed lightly over a completed project to maintain the fringe a little longer. It is entirely up to you whether or not you would like to try it out.

Hairbrush or comb. I use a detangling hairbrush for long or thick fringe and a fine-tooth comb to finish. I have also used a pet detangling comb, but you can use whatever works best for you.

Other natural materials like driftwood or shells pair perfectly with cotton for a beachy boho look.

Felt. I often use felt as a backing for projects that are designed to be hung on the wall. It provides structure and helps the finished piece maintain its shape. A stiffened felt is great if you can find it, but otherwise, regular craft felt is sufficient for most designs. A thick 3mm felt is required for large projects. I use a neutral cream color for most of my work but may use a dark tone if I've used dark cotton to complement it.

Floral wire. This is an alternative to felt to provide structure in a finished project.

Hanging rod. For wall hangings, you will need something to suspend them from. What you choose all depends on the look you want to achieve. Timber, dowels, driftwood, metallic piping, etc. all work well.

Clothes rack and hooks. I use these to suspend my wall hangings as I'm making them. They make the knotting process (which can take a few hours) more comfortable.

Needles. You will need a needle with a small eye (for yarn) and one with a large eye (for macramé cotton) to finish the wrapped projects.

Lark's Head Knot

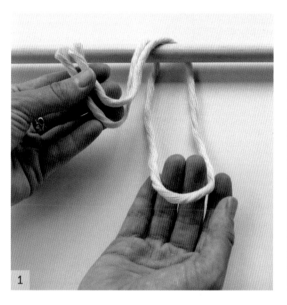

STEP 1: Fold. Fold or double over a length of cotton to form a loop in the middle. Pass the loop under the item you are attaching the cotton to, like a dowel, driftwood, wire, string, etc.

STEP 2: Finish. Bring the ends of the cotton around the dowel and through the loop. Pull to tighten. Repeat to attach additional pieces of cotton in the same manner.

MIX IT UP

The lark's head knot, also known as a slip knot, can be knotted on a dowel (shown in the step-by-step), driftwood, metallic rods, wire, another piece of cotton (as shown here), or anything else you would like. You can use it to vary your designs by having the front of the knot show in your finished project (left) or the back (right).

Square Knot

STEP 1: Bring the left strand over-under.
A square knot requires four strands of cotton. Here, I started with two lark's head knots to get the four strands I need. You will work with the two outermost strands. Bring the left strand over the two middle strands and under the right strand (over-under).

STEP 2: Bring the right strand under-over.
Now, bring the right strand behind (or under) the two middle strands and up and over the left strand (under–over). Pull tight. You have made a half knot.

STEP 3: Finish the knot. Now we are going to reverse the pattern. Bring the left strand under the middle two strands and over the right strand (under-over). Then bring the right strand over the middle two strands and down and under the left strand (over-under).

STEP 4: Pull tight. Pull this half knot tight against the one above it. Together, these two half knots make the square knot.

FOLLOWING THE PATTERN

Here's a simple rule or pattern to follow when making a square knot.
The first half of the knot will go over-under / under-over. The second half
of the knot will go under-over / over-under.

Clove Hitch or Double Half Hitch

STEP 1: Position the leading strand. I started with two lark's head knots so I have four strands. Take the strand on the left and pass it over the three remaining strands. This is the directional or the leading strand, and you will tie the other strands onto it.

STEP 2: Tie the first half hitch. Take the second strand on the left and pass it over and around the leading strand, bringing the end through the loop that has formed. Pull tight.

STEP 3: Tie the second half hitch. Repeat Step 2, using the same strand. Bring it over and around the leading strand and through the loop that forms. This second knot is what makes this a "double" half hitch. The second loop locks in the first one.

STEP 4: Repeat. Repeat Steps 2 and 3 with the remaining strands, using each one to tie two loops (half hitches) onto the leading strand to create one full knot (double half hitch).

CHOOSE YOUR SHAPE

Based on where you position the leading strand, you can use these knots to make all kinds of designs. You can make these knots diagonally, horizontally, in a semicircle, even in the shapes of leaves or vines. It all depends on that first leading strand and the direction you hold it in while knotting.

Basic Wrap

TOOLS & MATERIALS

Five pieces of macramé cotton (I used 5mm single-twist macramé cotton)

Any fiber for wrapping, like yarn, silk, or colored macramé cotton
(I used about 60´ [18m] of merino art yarn)

Scissors

Needle

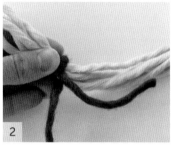

STEP 1: **Tie on the yarn.** Hold the pieces of 5mm cotton together and tie the yarn (or whatever material you are using for wrapping) around them at one end using a simple knot. Note, I've tied the yarn so there is a short tail in my left hand and a long tail for wrapping in my right hand.

STEP 2: **Start the wrap.** Fold the short end of the yarn over the knot toward the center of the cotton. Begin wrapping the long end of the yarn around the cotton and the short end of the yarn. This will secure the knot and hide the end of the yarn neatly.

STEP 3: **Continue wrapping.** Continue wrapping the yarn around the cotton. You want the wrap to be consistently tight but not so tight that it makes the cotton lumpy and uneven. Keep the wraps nice and close together so the cotton does not show through the yarn.

STEP 4: **Tie off the end.** When you reach the other end of the cotton, tie off the yarn by tucking the end under the last wrap and pulling it tight.

STEP 5: **Hide the end.** Thread a needle with the tail end of the yarn. Then, bring the needle through several wraps at the end of the cotton, bringing the end of the yarn with it. Pull the end of the yarn tight and trim it as close to the wraps as possible. This will hide and secure the knot and give your wrap a seamless finish.

Meditative Macramé

Tips for Maximizing the Wellness Potential of Knotting

Welcome to Macramé

There's a reason I have gotten hooked on this craft, and it is not just about making beautiful objects (although that's pretty fun, of course). Like many other crafts, macramé relies on a series of repetitive motions that can have a very soothing effect on body, mind, and spirit. As you work with the fiber to make knot after knot, you will find your hands and body in a relaxing rhythm. Try to notice that as you create. Soon, you will find yourself breathing deeply and feeling relaxed. It may take some time if you are new to the craft. But, the more you knot, the more you will find yourself getting immersed in your workflow, and you will turn to it frequently for a sense of calm.

Here are some quick tips for heightening the wellness benefits of macramé.

Find a suitable workspace: Find a well-lit or sunny location in your home, so you do not have to strain your eyes. Also, seek out a chair that will allow you to sit up straight while working to avoid neck or back pain.

Gather materials: Before you begin your macramé session, be sure you have enough fiber and everything you need. Nothing is more distracting than having to stop working to find more materials. Plan ahead.

Get comfortable: This is the fun part. Before you settle in, put on your favorite music, pour a cup of hot tea (or your favorite beverage), and wear some comfortable clothing. Consider this art session your time to engage in self-care. You deserve it.

Go with the "flow": Do you know that feeling you experience when you are so immersed in a task that time just slips away? That's called "flow," and it is good for you! As you work, try to focus on your breathing. Notice the texture of the fiber and admire your work as you go along. Be in the moment. Macramé can be incredibly meditative and have long-lasting benefits for you.

This serene room decorated with macramé feathers embodies the calm feeling I get while doing macramé. Find yourself a comfortable and well-lit place to work so you, too, can experience the relaxing benefits of macramé.

The Projects

Now that we have covered all the basics, it is time for you to put
your skills to work. This collection of projects includes all of my most
popular designs. My customers have loved them, and I know you will, too.
Remember that these pieces are also to inspire your own creativity.
I will walk you through my method for making each one, but you should
feel free to change the design or technique if you have a creative idea.
Have fun, and make each project your own!

Feathers & Leaves

These fluffy creations may remind you of feathers, or they may look more like leaves—it all depends on how you shape them. In this section, you will learn how to make a medium-sized feather and how to adapt the instructions to create a small and large version. I like to make multiple small feathers to display together, while the large feather makes a great stand-alone statement piece. Your color choice will also impact the look of the finished project. Neutral creams and light browns will mimic the look of feathers, while earthy saturated tones like greens, reds, or oranges will look more like leaves.

Feather

This medium-sized feather is perfect for learning this technique. Once you have mastered the process, follow the variation instructions to scale your feathers up or down. The trick to this design is thoroughly combing out the cotton strands. Brush and then comb your feather repeatedly from both the back and the front. Once the strands are smooth and manageable, you can shape your feather exactly as you want it.

TOOLS & MATERIALS

- 3mm single-twist macramé cotton in your preferred color:
  — One 37˝ (94cm) piece
  — Forty 11˝ (28cm) pieces
- 9˝ × 12˝ (A4) felt piece in neutral or cream for light-colored cotton and gray or another dark color for dark cotton

- Feather/Leaf pattern (see page 124)
- Scissors
- Tape measure
- Brush
- Comb
- Fabric glue

Feather, *continued*

STEP 1: Prepare the pieces. Trace the feather pattern onto the felt and cut it out. Cut all the lengths of cotton.

STEP 2: Knot the spine. Fold the longest (37″, 94cm) piece of cotton in half. Make a knot to form a small loop at the folded end. This will be the spine of the feather, and you will use the loop to hang up your finished project.

STEP 3: Start attaching the remaining strands. Starting at the looped end of the spine, use lark's head knots to attach the remaining pieces of cotton to it.

STEP 4: Finish attaching the remaining strands. Alternate the lark's head knots from one side of the spine to the other. Pull the knots tightly and firmly together as you work. I like to tie my knots so the backs are showing in the finished design (see below).

STEP 5: Knot the spine. Once all forty pieces of cotton have been added, use the two pieces of cotton from the spine to make a knot to hold everything in place.

STEP 6: Brush the sides. Using a detangling hairbrush, brush out both sides of the feather to unravel the cotton strands. Flip the feather over and repeat on the back side.

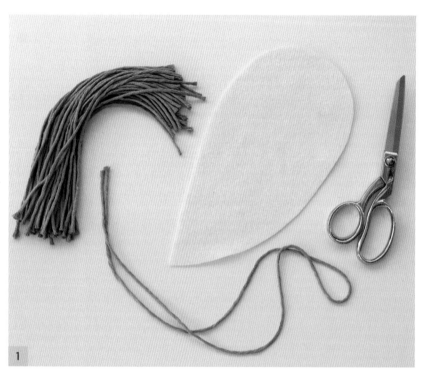

1

2

LARK'S HEAD KNOTS

In this design, I prefer to have the back of the lark's head knots showing on the front of the finished project (left). This makes the feather look more realistic than when the front of the knots are showing (right).

Feathers & Leaves

Feather, *continued*

STEP 7: **Comb the sides.** Once you've finished with the brush, comb through each side of the feather with a fine-tooth comb or brush to ensure the cotton strands are smooth and knot-free.

STEP 8: **Shape the feather.** Place the feather front (or right) side down. Comb through the cotton strands again, shaping them to match the felt backing piece as closely as possible.

STEP 9: **Apply the glue.** Apply clear-drying fabric glue to the felt backing and along the spine of the feather.

STEP 10: **Attach the felt.** Gently place the felt glue-side down onto the back of the feather, centering it as much as possible. Push down firmly for a few seconds. Then, turn the feather over briefly to ensure the felt or glue doesn't show through anywhere and make adjustments as needed.

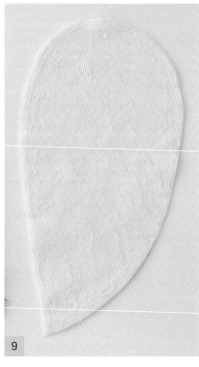

STEP 11: Trim from the back. This is the fun part! With the back of the feather facing up, trim around the edges, using the felt as a guide. I leave at least ¼" (6mm) of cotton extending past the felt edges.

STEP 12: Trim from the front. Place the feather right side up. Use the fine-tooth comb to comb through and shape the strands again. Then trim the edges as desired. Repeat until you are happy with the finished shape. Your feather is ready to be displayed! From time to time, you may need to re-comb it to maintain the shape and keep it neat and fluffy.

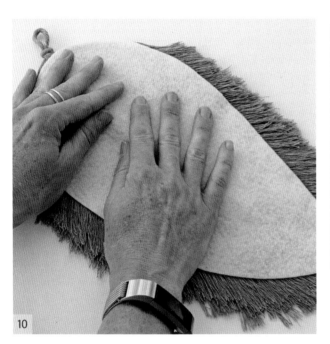

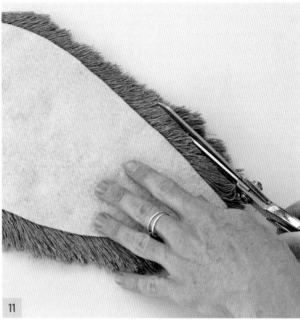

Small Feather

For this variation, you can leave out the felt backing. The feather will hold its shape just fine without it. Double over the longest piece of cotton and knot it in the center to form a loop (Steps 1–2). Use alternating lark's head knots to attach the remaining cotton pieces and make a knot in the spine after the last one (Steps 3–5). Brush, then comb the cotton strands and trim them to create the desired shape (Steps 6–8 and 11–12).

TOOLS & MATERIALS	• 3mm single-twist macramé cotton in your preferred color: — One 18˝ (46cm) piece — Sixteen 7˝ (18cm) pieces • Scissors • Tape measure • Brush • Comb

Large Feather

When I originally created this design, I essentially wanted to triple the size of the medium feather. Copy the feather pattern at 300% to create the large size. You can also sketch the shape freehand directly onto the felt. You will need a piece of felt about 27″ × 12″ to fit the large pattern (three A4 pieces placed side by side with the long edges together). Be sure to use 3mm-thick felt—the finished piece is heavy and will require more support than the medium feather. To make this variation, simply follow the steps for the medium feather using the materials listed below.

TOOLS & MATERIALS	• 5mm single-twist macramé cotton in your preferred color: — One 65″ (1.6m) piece — Sixty 22″ (56cm) pieces • 27″ × 12″ (68.5 x 30.5cm or three A4 pieces) piece of 3mm-thick felt in neutral or cream for light-colored cotton and gray or another dark color for dark cotton • Feather/Leaf pattern, copied at 300% (see page 124) • Scissors • Tape measure • Brush • Comb • Fabric glue

Knotted Coasters

Whether you are enjoying a hot cup of coffee or tea, an icy glass of lemonade, or a steaming bowl of soup, a good set of coasters will always come in handy. With macramé coasters, the knotted fiber provides a sturdy and thick barrier to protect your household surfaces. In this section, you will learn how to make coasters in three different shapes— heart, circle, and square. Choose whichever one best suits your taste and style, or try your hand at all three. You can even scale up the knotting pattern to turn them into placemats!

Heart Coaster

This heart design is cute and sweet, and a set of these coasters make an adorable gift for a friend. You could also design an extra-colorful set for your kids to use for a tea party. You will build the design using rows of square knots, forming one side of the heart, then the other, and bringing it all together at the bottom.

TOOLS & MATERIALS	
• Twelve 33˝ (84cm) pieces of 3mm single-twist macramé cotton in your preferred color • Dowel, coat hanger, or any straight, sturdy item	• Scissors • Tape measure • Comb

Heart Coaster, *continued*

STEP 1: Attach the cotton. Use lark's head knots to attach each piece of cotton to something stable and straight. I used a dowel attached to my benchtop, but you can use a coat hanger or anything sturdy that will allow you to maintain some tension on the cotton as you knot.

STEP 2: Knot the first row. Start knotting about 1˝ (2.5cm) below the dowel. The first row has two square knots, one on each side. Make the first square knot using the fifth and eighth strands on the left. Make the second square knot using the fifth and eighth strands on the right.

STEP 3: Knot the second row. The second row has four square knots, each building from the knots above. Make the first square knot using the third and sixth strands on the left. Make the second square knot using the seventh and tenth strands on the left. Repeat on the right side to make the third and fourth knots.

STEP 4: Knot the third row. The third row also builds out from the row above it with six square knots. Starting with the first and fourth strands on the left, make three square knots side by side. Repeat on the right side.

STEP 5: Knot the fourth row. For now, you have been knotting the two sides of the design separately. This row links both sides of the heart together. Starting with the third and sixth strands on the left, make five square knots side by side.

STEP 6: Knot the fifth row. Starting with the first and fourth strands on the left, make six square knots side by side. This will use all the strands and fill the entire row.

STEP 7: Knot the sixth row. Now you will begin to taper the knots to form the heart's point. Starting with the third and sixth strands on the left, make five square knots side by side.

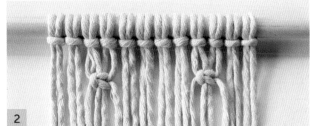

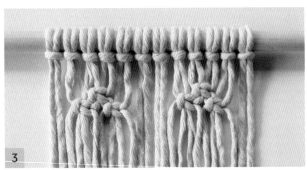

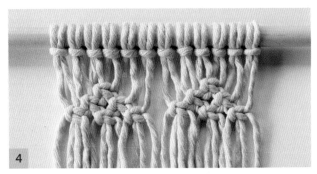

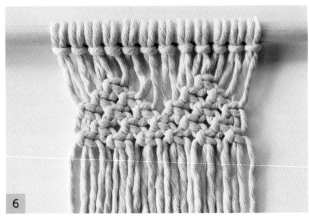

STEP 8: Knot the seventh row. Starting with the fifth and eighth strands on the left, make four square knots side by side.

STEP 9: Finish knotting the heart. For Row 8, start with the seventh and tenth strands on the left and make three square knots. For Row 9, start with the ninth and twelfth strands and make two square knots. For Row 10, use the eleventh and fourteenth strands to make one square knot.

STEP 10: Trim. Cut the loop at the front of each lark's head knot to remove the coaster from the dowel. Trim around the edges of the heart, leaving approximately 1˝ (2.5cm) of fringe. You can make the fringe longer or shorter depending on the look you want to achieve.

STEP 11: Finish the fringe. Using a fine-tooth comb, comb the fringe and trim again for a nice neat edge.

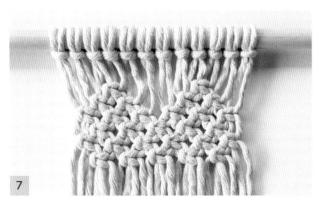

7

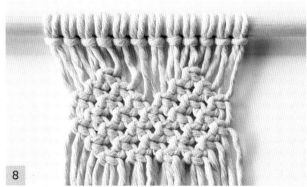

8

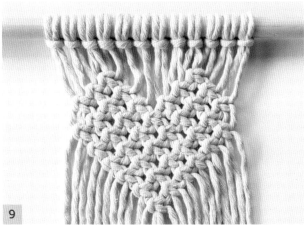

9

11

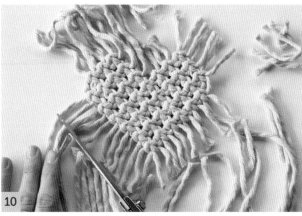

10

Circular Coaster

Now that you have mastered the heart design, a circle will be no problem. This is the perfect design to scale up for oversized mugs or bowls or to use as a trivet for serving dishes. Choose colors that match your kitchen or place settings. Remember that you can also change the look of your finished coasters by changing the length of the fringe. Leave it extra-long, trim it short, or anything in between!

TOOLS & MATERIALS	• Ten 33″ (84cm) pieces of 3mm single-twist macramé cotton in your preferred color • Dowel, coat hanger, or any straight, sturdy item	• Scissors • Tape measure • Comb

Circular Coaster, *continued*

STEP 1: Attach the cotton. Use lark's head knots to attach each piece of cotton to something stable and straight. I used a dowel attached to my benchtop, but you can use a coat hanger or anything sturdy that will allow you to maintain some tension on the cotton as you knot.

STEP 2: Knot the first row. Starting with the seventh and tenth strands on the left, make two square knots side by side.

STEP 3: Knot the second row. Starting with the fifth and eighth strands on the left, make three square knots side by side.

STEP 4: Knot the third row. Starting with the third and sixth strands on the left, make four square knots side by side.

STEP 5: Knot the fourth row. Starting with the first and fourth strands on the left, make five square knots side by side. This will use all the strands and fill the entire row.

STEP 6: Knot the fifth row. Starting with the third and sixth strands on the left, make four square knots side by side.

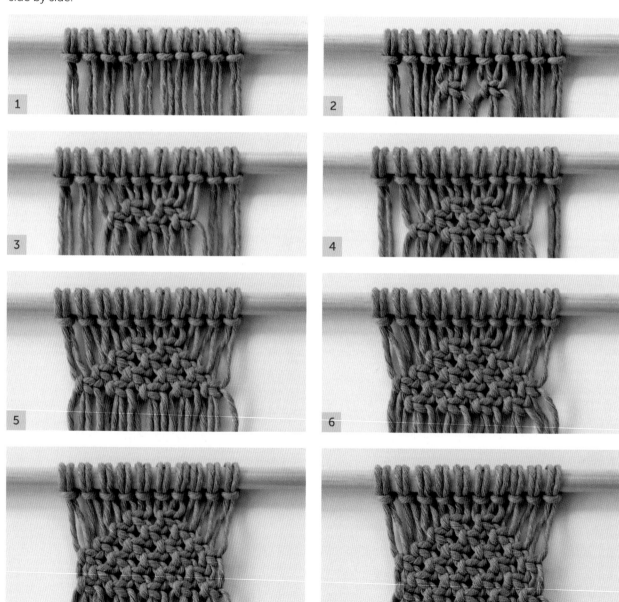

STEP 7: Knot the sixth row. Starting with the first and fourth strands on the left, make five square knots side by side.

STEP 8: Knot the seventh row. Starting with the third and sixth strands on the left, make four square knots side by side.

STEP 9: Knot the eighth row. Starting with the fifth and eighth strands on the left, make three square knots side by side.

STEP 10: Knot the ninth row. Starting with the seventh and tenth strands on the left, make two square knots side by side.

STEP 11: Trim. Cut the loop at the front of each lark's head knot to remove the coaster from the dowel. Trim around the edges of the circle, leaving approximately 1˝ (2.5cm) of fringe. You can make the fringe longer or shorter depending on the look you want to achieve.

STEP 12: Finish the fringe. Using a fine-tooth comb, comb the fringe and trim again for a nice neat edge.

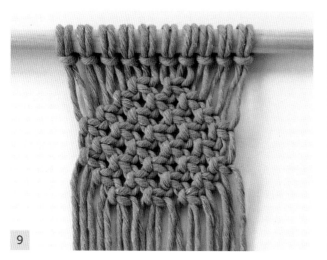

9

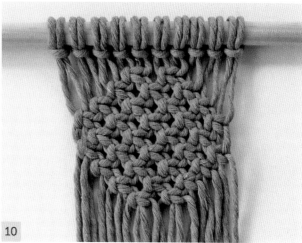

10

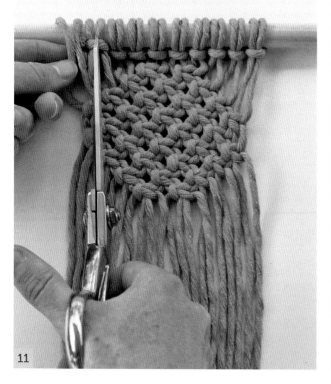

11

12

Square Coaster

If you want to go big with these coasters, a large version of this square design makes a perfect placemat. If you add extra rows, you can turn it into a rectangle. Challenge yourself to get creative with color. Try making a set of coasters in tints and shades of the same color, like several different shades of blue. Or try a color you don't usually gravitate toward. It may surprise you!

TOOLS & MATERIALS	
• Ten 33″ (84cm) pieces of 3mm single-twist macramé cotton in your preferred color	• Scissors
	• Tape measure
	• Comb
• Dowel, coat hanger, or any straight, sturdy item	

Square Coaster, *continued*

STEP 1: Attach the cotton. Use lark's head knots to attach each piece of cotton to something stable and straight. I used a dowel attached to my benchtop, but you can use a coat hanger or anything sturdy that will allow you to maintain some tension on the cotton as you knot.

STEP 2: Knot the first row. Starting with the first and fourth strands on the left, make five square knots side by side. This will use all the strands and fill the entire row.

STEP 3: Knot the second row. Starting with the third and sixth strands on the left, make four square knots side by side.

STEP 4: Knot the third row. Starting with the first and fourth strands on the left, make five square knots side by side.

STEP 5: Knot the fourth row. Starting with the third and sixth strands on the left, make four square knots side by side.

STEP 6: Knot the fifth row. Starting with the first and fourth strands on the left, make five square knots side by side.

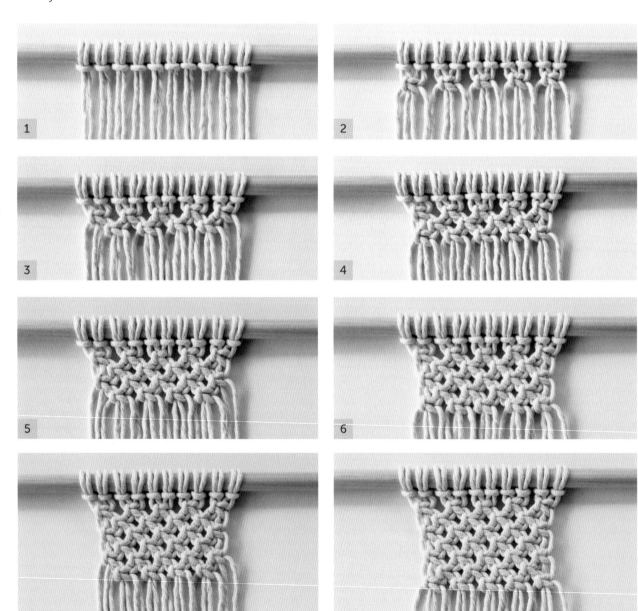

STEP 7: **Knot the sixth row.** Starting with the third and sixth strands on the left, make four square knots side by side.

STEP 8: **Knot the seventh row.** Starting with the first and fourth strands on the left, make five square knots side by side.

STEP 9: **Knot the eighth row.** Starting with the third and sixth strands on the left, make four square knots side by side.

STEP 10: **Knot the ninth row.** Starting with the first and fourth strands on the left, make five square knots side by side.

STEP 11: **Trim.** Cut the loop at the front of each lark's head knot to remove the coaster from the dowel. Trim the strands at the top and bottom of the square, leaving approximately 1″ (2.5cm) of fringe. You can make the fringe longer or shorter depending on the look you want to achieve.

STEP 12: **Finish the fringe.** Using a fine-tooth comb, comb the fringe and trim again for a nice neat edge.

9

10

11

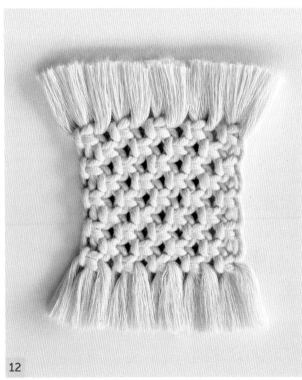
12

Charms

These charms are the perfect way to add a special touch to a gift or to add a bit of macramé flair to your home. In this section, you will learn to make a jar charm, a bouquet wrap, and a wall charm. The techniques used here are similar to those used for the Beachy Wall Hanging on page 108, just on a smaller scale, so they are a great way to practice. Once you have learned how to make each project, have fun discovering creative uses for them.

Jar Charm

I love to attach this finished piece to a candle, but it works well with any jar. I've often added them to jars of jam or jelly that I am giving as gifts. If this design matches your personal style, you may even want to try it as a statement necklace!

TOOLS & MATERIALS	• 3mm single-twist macramé cotton — One 28˝ (71cm) piece — Four 12˝ (30.5cm) pieces	• Scissors • Tape measure • Comb

Jar Charm, *continued*

STEP 1: Knot the ends. Tie a knot at each end of the 28˝ (71cm) string to prevent fraying.

STEP 2: Attach the remaining strands. Use lark's head knots to attach the remaining pieces of cotton to the 28˝ (71cm) piece.

STEP 3: Knot the first row. Starting with the first and fourth strands on the left, make two square knots side by side.

STEP 4: Knot the second row. Use the center four strands to tie a square knot in the middle of the design.

STEP 5: Start the V. Using the outer left strand as the leading strand, tie a clove hitch onto it with each of the three strands to the right.

STEP 6: Finish the V. Repeat on the right, tying a clove hitch onto the outer right strand with each of the three strands to the left. Then close the V with a fourth clove hitch.

STEP 7: Trim. Trim the strands at the bottom of the V, leaving approximately 1˝ (2.5cm) of fringe. You can make the fringe longer or shorter depending on the look you want to achieve.

STEP 8: Finish the fringe. Using a fine-tooth comb, comb the fringe and trim again for a nice neat edge.

5

6

7

8

Bouquet Wrap

Flowers are such a beautiful and thoughtful gift, and you can make them even more special with a beautiful macramé wrap. This design can be used to dress up a boho wedding bouquet or tied around a vase. The large size also makes it an excellent fit for wine bottles. What a unique way to package your gifts! This project uses lots of clove hitches to make the diamond shapes. If you need to practice the technique, check out page 20.

TOOLS & MATERIALS	
• 3mm single-twist macramé cotton — One 32˝ (81cm) piece — Twelve 28˝ (71cm) pieces • Two 8˝ (20.5cm) pieces of 5mm single-twist macramé cotton	• Scissors • Tape measure • Comb

Bouquet Wrap, *continued*

STEP 1: Knot the ends. Tie a knot at each end of the 32″ (81cm) string to prevent fraying.

STEP 2: Attach the short strands. Use lark's head knots to attach the 28″ (71cm) pieces of cotton to the 32″ (81cm) piece.

STEP 3: Knot the first row. Starting with the first and fourth strands on the left, make six square knots side by side.

STEP 4: Knot the second row. Use the third and sixth strands on the left to tie a square knot. Skip four strands and tie a second square knot. Skip four strands and tie a third square knot.

STEP 5: Make the Vs. Using the outer left strand as the leading strand, tie a clove hitch onto it with each of the three strands to the right. Using the eighth strand on the left as the leading strand, tie a clove hitch onto it with each of the three strands to the left. Close the V with a fourth clove hitch. Repeat with the next set of eight strands, then with the remaining set of eight strands. When finished, you will have three Vs.

STEP 6: Make the tops of the diamonds. Using the ninth strand on the left as the leading strand. tie a clove hitch onto it with each of the four strands to the left. Using the ninth strand again, tie a clove hitch onto it with each of the three strands to the right. Repeat

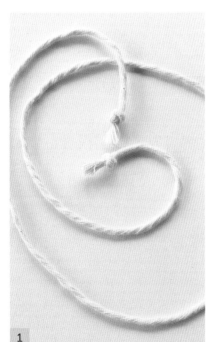

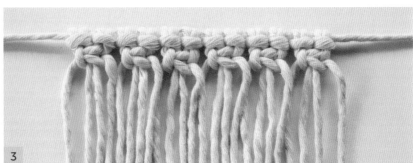

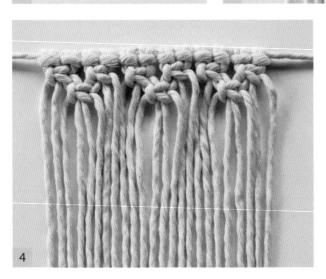

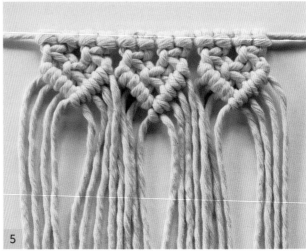

with the seventeenth strand on the left to form the top of the second diamond.

STEP 7: **Make the bottoms of the diamonds.** Using the fifth strand on the left as the leading strand, tie a clove hitch onto it with each of the three strands to the right. Using the twelfth strand on the left as the leading strand, tie a clove hitch onto it with each of the three strands to the left. Close the diamond with a fourth clove hitch. Repeat with the thirteenth and twentieth strands on the left to finish the second diamond.

STEP 8A and 8B: **Attach the tassels.** Take a piece of 5mm cotton and push the ends through the left diamond from front to back, on either side of the center strands. Now bring both ends of the cotton through the diamond from back to front, between the center strands. Repeat with the remaining 5mm cotton and the right diamond.

STEP 9: **Finish the tassels.** Trim each tassel to about 1″ (2.5cm) long. Using a fine-tooth comb, comb the tassels and trim again for a nice neat edge.

6

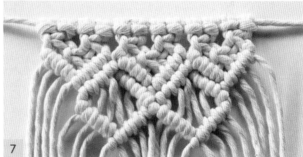

7

8A

9

8B

Wall Charm

If you'd like to add a little macramé style to your walls but aren't quite ready to tackle a full-size wall hanging, this is the perfect place to start. It is a really simple way to make a mini wall hanging. You don't need anything special to hang it on like a dowel or driftwood, just cotton. You can get creative with the design if you like and even make a large banner-style hanging by repeating the pattern and using longer pieces of cotton.

| TOOLS & MATERIALS | • 5mm single-twist macramé cotton
— One 15″ (38cm) piece
— Six 30″ (76cm) pieces | • Scissors
• Tape measure
• Comb |

Wall Charm, *continued*

STEP 1: Attach the strands. Use lark's head knots to attach the long pieces of cotton to the short 15″ (38cm) piece.

STEP 2: Tie the square knots. Using the four left strands, tie three square knots.

STEP 3: Pull the strands through. Make a space above the square knots between the center strands. Bring the two center strands at the bottom of the square knots up and through the space from front to back.

STEP 4: Pull tight. Pull the center strands tight. This will roll up the series of square knots you made in Step 2, forming a ball.

STEP 5: Tie a square knot. To hold the ball in place, tie a square knot with the four left strands. The end result is called a berry knot.

STEP 6: Repeat. Repeat Steps 2–5 with the next set of four strands, then the remaining four strands.

STEP 7: **Knot the second row.** Starting with the third and sixth strands on the left, tie two square knots side by side.

STEP 8: **Knot the third row.** Using the four center strands, tie a square knot.

STEP 9: **Make the V.** Using the outer left strand as the leading strand, tie a clove hitch onto it with each of the five strands to the right. Repeat on the right, tying a clove hitch onto the outer right strand with each of

the five strands to the left. Close the V with a sixth clove hitch.

STEP 10: **Trim.** Trim the strands at the bottom of the V, leaving approximately 1″ (2.5cm) of fringe. You can make the fringe longer or shorter depending on the look you want to achieve.

STEP 11: **Finish the fringe.** Using a fine-tooth comb, comb the fringe and trim again for a nice neat edge.

8

9

10

11

Tassel

So fluffy and so fun. Tassels have lots of personality packed into a simple, small design. Tassels make fun charms for key rings or necklaces, or you can string them onto a long piece of cotton for a unique garland. You can really change the look of a tassel by using different colors, fibers, materials, thickness, and lengths, or even by attaching gemstones, shells, stones, or other items. Let your creativity run wild with this adorable project!

TOOLS & MATERIALS	• 4 to 5 pieces of 3mm or 5mm single-twist macramé cotton in any length	• Scissors
		• Tape measure
		• Comb
	• Key ring (optional)	

Tassel, *continued*

STEP 1: Secure the strands. Set aside a long piece of cotton. Take the remaining cotton pieces and place them together in a bundle. If you're using a key ring, thread it onto the cotton pieces, positioning it in the center. If you're not using a key ring, take one of the cotton pieces and tie it around the center of the bundle. This is your tassel.

STEP 2: Comb. Comb out the strands of the tassel.

STEP 3: Start the wrap. Take the long piece of cotton you set aside in Step 1. Hold one end in place near the top of the tassel. Then, fold the cotton to make a loop on top of the tassel and hold it in place.

STEP 4: Wrap the tassel. Take the long end of the cotton and wrap it tightly around the top of the tassel and the loop you made in Step 3. Continue wrapping the tassel until you are happy with the way it looks (wrap it at least three times to keep it tight). Do not cover the loop completely. A portion of it should remain sticking out of the bottom of the wrap.

STEP 5: Secure the end. Once you are happy with the wrap, bring the long end of the cotton through the loop at the bottom of the wrap. Now, start tightening the loop by pulling on the other end of the cotton at the top of the tassel.

STEP 6: Tighten. Keep tightening the loop until it disappears into the wrap, pulling the long end of the cotton with it. Pull tight on both ends of the cotton and then trim them close to the wrap.

STEP 7: Finish. Comb your tassel again, trim it to the desired length, and you are done!

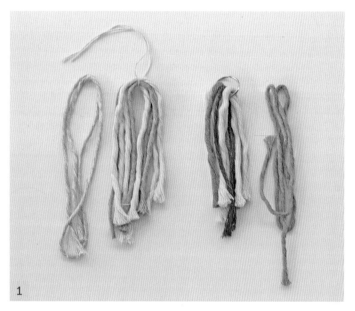

1

2

WRAPPED KNOTS

The wrapped knot, also known as a gathering knot, is a simple flat knot that secures and hides both ends of the tassel wrap nicely (left). Another option is to wrap the top of the tassel, tie the cotton ends in a double knot, and incorporate them into your tassel by combing them out (right).

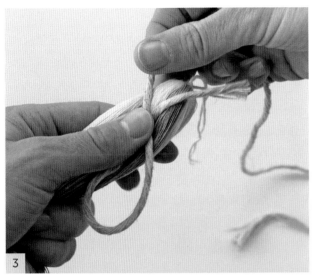

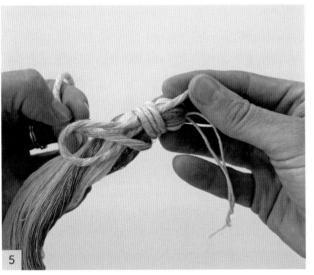

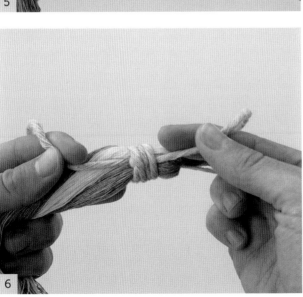

Wrapped Rainbows

I love these wrapped rainbows! They are a wonderful way to introduce a bit of cheer and whimsy into any room in your home—I think that's one of the reasons I'm asked about them so often. These designs are also super easy to customize to match your personal style. Simply choose colors that you love or that match the décor in your home. In this section, you will learn how to make rainbows in three different sizes, so no matter what you want to use them for, you will have the perfect design to match.

Mini Rainbow

How cute is this tiny design? It makes a great gift to brighten someone's day, or you can make several at a time for party favors. The instructions here will show you how to make a charm for your bag, but you can easily use your finished rainbows for jewelry or other projects (see more about this on page 73). When you are making this design, remember to refer to the wrapping technique on page 21.

TOOLS & MATERIALS		
	• Yarn in 3 different colors (you will need about 19 ½"–23½" [50–60cm] of each color)	• Lobster claw swivel clasp
		• Scissors
	• Three 7½" (19cm) pieces of single-twist macramé cotton (I used 5.5mm string)	• Tape measure
		• Comb
		• Fabric glue
	• One 10" (25.5cm) piece of sturdy macramé cotton (I used 1.5mm polished cotton)	• Needle

Mini Rainbow, *continued*

STEP 1: Attach the thin cotton. Attach the 1.5mm cotton string to the loop of the clasp using a lark's head knot. Then secure it with a clove hitch.

STEP 2: Attach the thick cotton. Apply a bit of fabric glue to the base of the clove hitch and partway down each strand. Press the center of one of the remaining pieces of cotton onto the glue and hold until secure.

STEP 3: Wrap the cotton. Take a piece of yarn and tie it around the left strands of cotton (both the 1.5mm and 5.5mm pieces) about 1¼˝ (3cm) from the clasp. Working toward the clasp, wrap the yarn around the cotton, hiding the short end of the yarn as you go. When you reach the clasp, continue the wrap onto the right strands of cotton until you've covered about 1¼˝ (3cm).

STEP 4: Finish the end. Tie off the yarn at the end of the wrap leaving a tail. Use a needle to hide the end of the yarn in the wrap and trim it.

STEP 5: Wrap the remaining cotton pieces. Use another color of yarn to wrap the center of one of the remaining cotton pieces. To determine how long the wrap should be, nestle the cotton inside the first piece to see if the wraps will match up with one another when formed into the rainbow shape and adjust as needed. Repeat with the third piece of cotton and the remaining yarn color.

STEP 6: Glue the first row. You can glue or sew the rows of your rainbow together. I used glue. Fold the bottom (smallest) row of the rainbow in half and use glue to secure it in place. If you use too much glue, wipe off the excess. You need enough glue to hold the cotton together but not so much that it oozes out the sides. Hold it in place for a few minutes (or use a clip) until the glue has dried.

STEP 7: Glue the second row. Add a small line of glue to the top edge of the rainbow's bottom row and attach the second row. Hold the pieces in place until the glue dries.

STEP 8: Glue the third row. Repeat to glue the top row of the rainbow in place.

STEP 9: Comb. Once all the glue is completely dry (about 10 minutes), comb out the cotton strands at the bottom of the rainbow. Then trim them to finish.

Mini Rainbow Earrings

You can use a very similar technique to turn the mini rainbow into a pair of earrings. Skip Steps 1–2 because you won't need to attach a clasp. Instead, follow Steps 3–9 to wrap each piece of cotton with yarn and glue them together. Then, attach your preferred earring findings. I used sterling silver jump rings to attach an earring hook to each rainbow. I threaded a ring through the yarn at the top row of a rainbow and then through an earring hook. You may need to use jewelry pliers depending on the type of earring finding you choose.

TOOLS & MATERIALS	
• 6 strands of yarn, 2 each of 3 different colors (you will need about 15˝ [38cm] of each color)	• Scissors
	• Tape measure
	• Comb
• Six 5½˝ (14cm) pieces of single-twist macramé cotton (I used 5mm string)	• Fabric glue
	• Needle
• Two earring findings of your choice	• Jewelry pliers (optional)

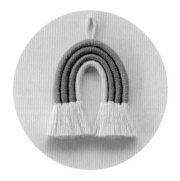

Small Rainbow

This design looks adorable in multiples. Make several in different colors to create a collage on your wall or turn them into a mobile for a nursery. These make adorable gifts for kids and adults alike!

TOOLS & MATERIALS	
• Yarn in 3 different colors (you will need up to 6½′ [2m] of each color) • Three 9½″ (24cm) pieces of single-twist macramé cotton (I used 9mm string) • One 3″ (7.5cm) piece of macramé cotton (I used 3mm single-twist macramé cotton)	• Felt in a neutral color • Small rainbow pattern (see page 127) • Scissors • Tape measure • Comb • Fabric glue • Needle

Small Rainbow, *continued*

STEP 1: Make the hanger. Trace the small rainbow pattern onto the felt and cut it out. Fold the 3″ (7.5cm) piece of cotton in half to form a loop and glue it to the top of the felt arch to make a hanger.

STEP 2: Wrap the first piece of cotton. Tie a piece of yarn onto a remaining cotton piece about 1½″ (4cm) from one end. Use the yarn to wrap the cotton, covering the short end of the yarn as you go. Wrap until you are about 1½″ (4cm) from the other end of the cotton. Tie off the yarn leaving a tail.

STEP 3: Finish the end. Use a needle to hide the tail end of the yarn in the wrap and trim it.

STEP 4: Wrap the remaining cotton pieces. Repeat Steps 2–3 to wrap each of the remaining cotton pieces in a different color of yarn. Nestle the cotton pieces inside one another to determine how long the wraps

need to be to match up with one another when formed into the rainbow shape. Also, use the felt backing to guide you on the size and shape you want to achieve.

STEP 5: Glue the rows together. Nestle the rows of the rainbow together and form them into the rainbow shape. Apply a good layer of fabric glue to the felt backing. Once you are happy with the rainbow rows' shape and position, firmly press the felt in place on top of them.

STEP 6: Trim. The fabric glue will take a few minutes to dry. While it does, check the front of the rainbow to make sure the rows are symmetrical and firmly pushed together. Make any adjustments needed before the glue dries. Once you are happy and the glue has dried, trim the ends of the cotton even, comb out the strands, and trim them again for an even edge.

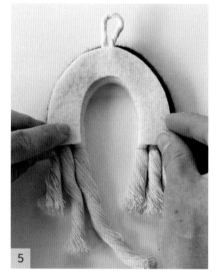

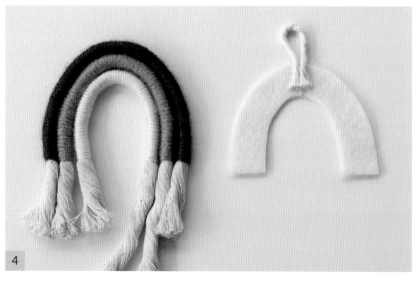

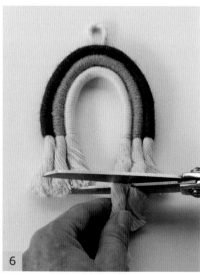

Extra Rows

You can add additional rows/colors to your rainbow—you will just need to alter the felt backing to accommodate them. Each row is just over ⅛″ (5mm) wide. Use this to make the felt backing as large as you need it. You can also wrap the rainbow rows and then trace them onto the felt to get the right size for the backing. Follow the steps for the small rainbow to wrap the rows and glue them in place.

TOOLS & MATERIALS	
• Yarn, 1 color for each row of the rainbow (you will need up to 6½′ [2m] of each color) • 9½″ (24cm) pieces of single-twist macramé cotton (I used 9mm string), 1 for each row of the rainbow • One 3″ (7.5cm) piece of macramé cotton (I used 3mm single-twist macramé cotton)	• Felt in a neutral color • Small rainbow pattern, adjusted to fit the extra rows (see page 127) • Scissors • Tape measure • Comb • Fabric glue • Needle

Large Rainbow

If you like big statement pieces, this oversized rainbow is for you. It is perfect for hanging over a desk or bed, even in a kids' bathroom. With this large design, you might want to make the fringe extra-long and play around with some fun additions like beads or jewels.

TOOLS & MATERIALS	
• 3mm single-twist macramé cotton in 3 different colors for wrapping (you will need up to 17½′ [5.3m] of each color)	• Felt in a neutral color
	• Large rainbow pattern (see page 126)
• Fifteen 26″ (66cm) pieces of single-twist macramé cotton (I used 5mm string)	• Scissors
	• Tape measure
	• Brush/comb (optional)
• One 5″ (13cm) piece of macramé cotton (I used 3mm single-twist macramé cotton)	• Fabric glue
	• Needle

Large Rainbow, *continued*

STEP 1: Make the hanger. Trace the large rainbow pattern onto the felt and cut it out. Fold the 5″ (13cm) piece of cotton in half to form a loop and glue it to the top of the felt arch to make a hanger.

STEP 2: Wrap the first row. Hold five pieces of the 5mm cotton together and tie a piece of colored cotton around them about 3″ (7.5cm) from one end. Use the colored cotton to wrap the 5mm cotton pieces, covering the short end of the colored cotton as you go. Wrap until you are about 3″ (7.5cm) from the other end of the 5mm cotton pieces. Tie off the colored cotton leaving a tail.

STEP 3: Finish the end. Use a needle to hide the tail end of the colored cotton in the wrap and trim it.

STEP 4: Wrap the remaining cotton pieces. Repeat Steps 2–3 to wrap each of the remaining rainbow rows in a different color of cotton. Nestle the rows inside one another to determine how long the wraps need to be to match up with one another when formed into the rainbow shape. Also, use the felt pattern to guide you on the size and shape you want to achieve.

STEP 5: Glue the rows together. Nestle the rainbow rows together and form them into the rainbow shape. Apply a good layer of fabric glue to the felt backing. Once you are happy with the rainbow rows' shape and position, firmly press the felt in place on top of them.

STEP 6: Trim. The fabric glue will take a few minutes to dry. While it does, check the front of the rainbow to make sure the rows are symmetrical and firmly pushed together. Make any adjustments needed before the glue dries. Once you are happy and the glue has dried, trim the ends of the cotton even. You can leave the fringe as is or brush/comb out the strands to make them fluffy. If you brush out the strands, trim them afterward for an even edge.

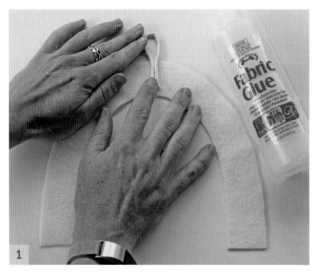

Extra Rows

As with the small rainbow, you can add additional rows/colors to your large rainbow. You just need to alter the felt backing to accommodate them. Each row is just over ⅜˝ (10mm) wide. Use this to make the felt backing as large as you need it. You can also wrap the rainbow rows and then trace them onto the felt to get the right size for the backing. Follow the steps for the large rainbow to wrap the rows and glue them in place.

TOOLS & MATERIALS	
• 3mm single-twist macramé cotton, 1 color for each row of the rainbow (you will need up to 17½˝ [5.3m] of each color)	• Felt in a neutral color
	• Large rainbow pattern, adjusted to fit the extra rows (see page 126)
• 26˝ (66cm) pieces of single-twist macramé cotton (I used 5mm string), 5 pieces for each row of the rainbow	• Scissors
	• Tape measure
	• Brush/comb (optional)
• One 5˝ (13cm) piece of macramé cotton (I used 3mm single-twist macramé cotton)	• Fabric glue
	• Needle

Decorative Knots

These decorative knots are a wonderful way to show off your macramé skills. While the end result is stunning, they are simple and fun to make. In this section, you'll learn to make three of my favorites—the Pipa, Josephine, and cloud knots. Each knot can be made with a single strand of cotton, or you can double or triple the cotton strands for a thicker knot (see the sample photos for the Josephine and cloud knots). In the tutorials, I've chosen to use a wrapped piece of cotton to make my knots oversized and chunky. If you'd like to do the same, follow the instructions on page 21 to make a wrapped piece of cotton to use for these knots.

Pipa Knot

This knot has a nautical look that I really love. Using a wrapped piece of cotton (see the instructions on page 21) gives it lots of dimension, too. But remember that you can also use a single piece of cotton to tie the knot, especially if you would like some practice to master the technique.

TOOLS & MATERIALS	• Wrapped piece of cotton (see page 21) • Scissors • Fabric glue (optional)

Pipa Knot, *continued*

STEP 1: Make the first loop. Take one end of your cotton and create a small loop, as shown. One end lies flat with the long working end on top.

STEP 2: Make the second loop. Take the working end and create a big loop below the first one. The knot should resemble a figure 8. The working end should be on the left side.

STEP 3: Wrap the top. Wrap the working end around the small loop as shown.

STEP 4: Make another loop. Make another loop at the bottom of the knot, fitting it inside the large loop. The working end should finish on the left side.

STEP 5: **Wrap the top.** Wrap the working end around the top of the knot, below the wrap you made in Step 3.

STEP 6: **Repeat.** Repeat Steps 4–5 as many times as needed to fill the large loop at the bottom of the knot with increasingly smaller loops.

STEP 7: **Finish.** When you can't add any more loops, bring the working end through the center of the smallest loop from front to back. Your knot is complete! It will hold its shape as it is, but for extra security, you can glue or stitch the ends in place if you like.

5

6

7

CREATIVE COLOR WRAPS

When creating a wrap, you don't have to limit yourself to one color. Use multiple colors to make a fun pattern (as shown on page 85) or even an ombré look. Have fun experimenting!

Josephine Knot

This knot is very popular—you've probably seen it before in jewelry designs. I think this large version makes a great wall charm. Make it with a single piece of cotton or a wrapped piece of cotton (see page 21). If you want to get really creative, try using three strands of cotton, each in a different color, as shown in the sample photo. Tie the knot with one piece of cotton first, making it extra loose and big. Then add the second piece of cotton, following the first, and so on.

TOOLS & MATERIALS	• Wrapped piece of cotton (see page 21)
	• Scissors
	• Comb (optional)

Josephine Knot, *continued*

STEP 1: Fold the cotton. Fold the cotton in half, making a long loop in the center, as shown.

STEP 2: Make the first loop. Take the left working end and make a loop on top of the center loop, as shown.

STEP 3: Weave the right working strand. Bring the right working end around the bottom of the knot and over the left working end. Then, weave it through the strands, bringing it under the center loop, then over, under, and over the subsequent strands as shown.

STEP 4: Finish. Pull the ends of the cotton to tighten the knot. You may have to tighten the loops of the knot one at a time, following them through the knot, pulling them tight as you go, to make everything snug. Trim the ends to your desired length. You can comb out the cotton strands or leave them as is.

DRESS IT UP

A double Josephine knot with an
extra-large center loop makes a beautiful,
unique necklace or wall charm.

Cloud Knot

While the Pipa knot has a nautical style, this design reminds me of Celtic knot patterns. Like the Josephine knot, it really looks impressive with two or three strands of cotton as shown in the sample photo, or you can use a wrapped piece of cotton for an open, chunky look.

TOOLS & MATERIALS	• Wrapped piece of cotton (see page 21)
	• Scissors
	• Comb (optional)

Cloud Knot, *continued*

STEP 1: Reverse the weave. This knot starts with a completed Josephine knot (follow the instructions on page 90). Undo the last weave on each side of the knot. This means the left working end should pass over two strands in a row (instead of over-under), and the right working end should pass under two strands in a row (instead of under-over) as shown.

STEP 2: Weave the left working end. Take the left working end and weave it through the strands at the bottom right of the knot, bringing it over, under, over as shown. Be sure to keep the knot flat and leave lots of space in the loops as you work.

STEP 3: Weave the right working end. Take the right working end and weave it through the strands at the bottom left of the knot, bringing it over, under, over, under as shown. Be sure to keep the knot flat and leave lots of space in the loops as you work.

STEP 4: Finish. Pull the ends of the cotton to tighten the knot. You may have to tighten the loops one at a time, following them through the knot, pulling them tight as you go, to make everything snug. Trim the ends to your desired length. You can comb out the cotton strands or leave them as is.

Cloud Knot Bracelet

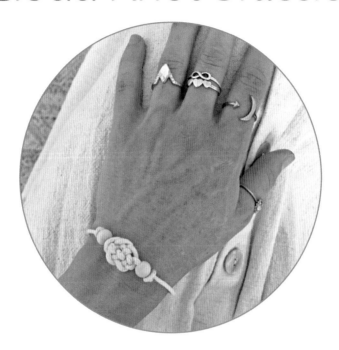

A mini version of the cloud knot, made with thin macramé cotton, makes a cute bracelet or anklet. Cut the cotton to length. You'll need it to be long enough to fit around your wrist or ankle with some extra to account for the knot and to give yourself some wiggle room. You can always trim the ends of the cotton when you've finished the bracelet. Tie a cloud knot directly in the center of the cotton. Thread a bead onto each end of the cotton and use single knots to secure them against the cloud knot. Knot each end of the cotton to prevent fraying. It's ready to wear!

TOOLS & MATERIALS	• Approximately 19½″ (50cm) of 2.5mm polished cotton string, depending on the size of your wrist/ankle
	• Two 8mm wooden beads
	• Scissors
	• Measuring tape

Boho Flower

This pattern only uses one knot—the clove hitch. But with that one knot, you can make a variety of petals to form different types of macramé flowers. I will demonstrate one petal shape with this project. Once you master it, you can get creative with different shapes and sizes for your petals.

TOOLS & MATERIALS	• Six 33˝ (84cm) pieces of single-twist macramé cotton per petal (I used 30 pieces of 3mm string to make 5 petals) • Scrap material like macramé cotton or another fiber for the flower center	• Scissors • Tape measure

Boho Flower, *continued*

STEP 1: Prepare the pieces. Lay five of the cotton pieces side by side, positioning them horizontally. Fold the sixth piece in half and place the folded end over the middle of the other pieces, positioning it vertically.

STEP 2: Make the first clove hitch. The ends of the folded string will be the leading strands for the clove hitches. Use the right end of the top string to tie a clove hitch on the right leading strand.

STEP 3: Make the second clove hitch. Repeat on the left side, using the top string's left end to tie a clove hitch on the left leading strand.

STEP 4: Repeat. Repeat with the remaining pieces of cotton, using the right end of each one to tie a clove hitch onto the right leading strand and the left end of each one to tie a clove hitch onto the left leading strand.

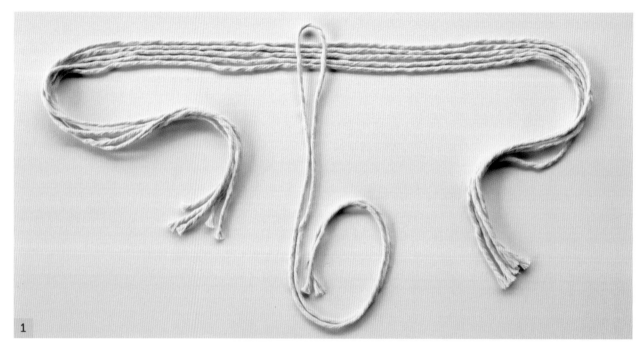

STEP 5: **Close the petal.** To bring the bottom of the petal together, use the left leading strand to tie a clove hitch onto the right leading strand. Once you have finished the knot, position the leading strands so you have six strands on each side of the petal.

STEP 6: **Position the leading strand.** Place the top left strand over the remaining five strands on the left side. This is now the leading strand.

STEP 7: **Tie a clove hitch.** Use the top left strand to tie a clove hitch on the left leading strand.

STEP 8: **Repeat.** Repeat with the remaining strands on the left side, using each one to tie a clove hitch onto the left leading strand.

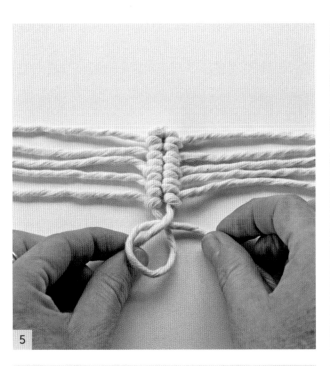

Boho Flower, *continued*

STEP 9: Repeat on the right side. Repeat Steps 6–8 on the right side of the design. Then, bring the bottom of the petal together by using the left leading strand to tie a clove hitch on the right leading strand. Position the leading strands so you have six strands on each side of the petal.

STEP 10: Add a final row. Repeat Steps 6–9 to add another row of clove hitches to each side of the petal and close the bottom. Your flower petal is complete!

STEP 11: Make more petals. Follow the steps to make four more petals so you have five total.

STEP 12: Connect two petals. Place two petals next to each other, front sides down, and tie the adjacent strands together using double knots. To keep the flower from curling inward, don't tie the top set of strands together. Instead, tie the second set of strands around them.

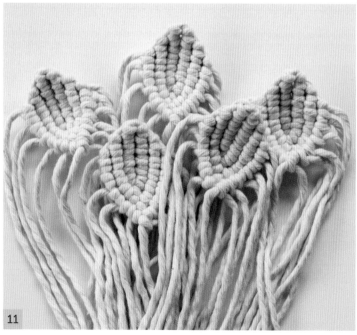

STEP 13: Check your work. When finished, you should have five knots down the seam between the petals with the top set of strands tucked into the first knot. This is the view from the front.

STEP 14: Attach the remaining petals. Repeat to connect the remaining petals.

STEP 15: Finish. Knot or loop the scraps of fiber and thread them through the center of the flower. Trim the ends or use them to make a loop to hang your flower on the wall or to tie it around a vase, candle, or bouquet.

Sun Mandala

Metal hoops and embroidery hoops have become popular bases for floral arrangements. This project allows you to create similar wall décor, but with a knotted design instead of flowers. I used a 6″ (15cm) ring for this project, but you can use a larger or smaller ring depending on the look you are going for. You will just need longer pieces of cotton if you size up.

TOOLS & MATERIALS	
• 3mm single-twist macramé cotton: — Forty to fifty 8″ (20.5cm) pieces — One 40″ (1m) piece • Four 26″ (66cm) pieces of natural 5mm single-twist macramé cotton • Four 10′ (3m) pieces of colored 3mm single-twist macramé cotton, each in a different color	• 6″ (15cm)-diameter metal ring • Scissors • Tape measure • Comb • Fabric glue

STEP 1: Start attaching the fringe. Using lark's head knots, attach about ten 8″ (20.5) pieces of cotton to the metal ring. Use a lark's head knot to attach the 40″ (1m) piece of cotton to the ring. Adjust the ends so the one furthest from the other pieces is short (matching the rest of the fringe) and the end closest to the other pieces is very long.

STEP 2: Start tying clove hitches. Use the long piece of cotton as a leading strand. Place it against the outside edge of the ring and tie a clove hitch onto it with each fringe piece.

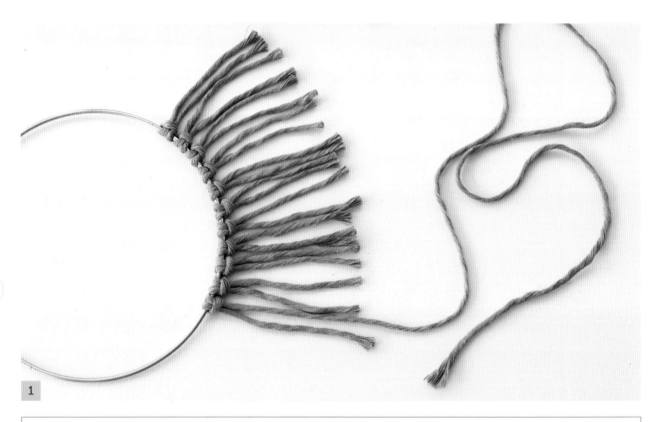

1

TIP

It can be tricky to wrap a thin piece of cotton like the 5mm string we are using for this project. You may find it easier to hold the cotton you are wrapping against something more stable, like a piece of floral wire, as you wrap. When you've finished wrapping, simply pull the wire out of the wrap.

STEP 3: Finish adding the fringe. Continue working around the ring, adding more 8″ (20.5) pieces of cotton using lark's head knots and locking them in place with clove hitches. Repeat until you have gone around the ring completely. You should finish by tying the short end of the 40″ (1m) cotton piece from Step 1 onto the leading strand with a clove hitch.

STEP 4: Start the first wrap. Take a 26″ (66cm) piece of cotton and begin wrapping it with a colored piece of cotton. Start the wrap about 2″ (5cm) from one end.

STEP 5: Finish the wrap. Tie off the wrap about 2″ (5cm) from the end of the natural cotton. Leave the tail end of the colored cotton loose; do not thread it back through the wrap as you will use it in the next step.

2

3

4

Sun Mandala, *continued*

STEP 6: **Connect the ends.** Make sure the wrapped cotton fits snuggly inside the metal ring. You may need to make adjustments to the length of the wrap. Once you are sure that it is sized properly, tie the tail ends of the colored cotton together over both ends of the natural cotton in a simple single knot, forming a ring.

STEP 7: **Trim.** Trim the ends of the cotton, leaving short tails.

STEP 8: **Attach the first ring.** Apply a thin line of fabric glue along the inner edge of the metal ring. Then firmly press the wrapped ring in place.

STEP 9: **Repeat.** Repeat Steps 4–8 with the remaining pieces of cotton. As you attach the wrapped rings, stagger the tail ends of the natural cotton so they are spaced several inches apart along one side of the metal ring.

STEP 10: **Finish.** Comb out the fringe around the outside of the ring, and the tail ends of the wrapped cotton. Trim the fringe for an even edge around the ring. When finished, you can easily use a small nail to hang this on the wall. A nail will easily slide through one of the spaces between the lark's head knots.

9

10

Beachy Wall Hanging

This is the ultimate macramé project—a beautiful, big, beachy wall hanging. But do not let the size or the design intimidate you. This project uses the same knots you have used for every other project in this book, and it is broken down into sections so you can build it one piece at a time. This design has lots of long fringe that you can trim creatively or adorn with beads, shells, or other items. Have fun testing your macramé skills with this design!

TOOLS & MATERIALS	
• 3mm single-twist macramé cotton: — Four 70″ (1.8m) pieces — One 60″ (1.5m) piece — Four 11½′ (3.5m) pieces — Six 10′ (3m) pieces — Twenty-eight 44″ (1.1m) pieces (optional: substitute recycled silk for 4 of the pieces) — Sixteen 25″ (63.5cm) pieces	— Sixteen 16″ (40.5cm) pieces — About sixteen 5″ (13cm) pieces • Hanging rod (I used driftwood) • Natural wooden beads and shells (optional) • Scissors • Tape measure • Comb

Beachy Wall Hanging, *continued*

STEP 1: **Hang the rod.** Hang up the driftwood (or whatever material you are using) so you have enough room to work. I use hooks suspended from a clothes rack to hold my wall hangings as I knot them.

STEP 2: **Attach the first piece of cotton.** This wall hanging is built in sections. We will start with the center semicircle. Attach one of the 70˝ (1.8m) cotton pieces to the driftwood with a lark's head knot.

STEP 3: **Tie a clove hitch.** Use the right strand to tie a clove hitch onto the left strand.

STEP 4: **Add two strands.** Attach two more 70˝ (1.8m) strands to the driftwood using lark's head knots, one on each side of the clove hitch.

STEP 5: **Tie the first row.** Use the second strand on the left as the leading stand. Tie a clove hitch onto the leading strand with each strand to the right.

STEP 6: **Tie the second row.** Using the far right strand as the leading strand, tie a clove hitch onto it with each strand to the left.

STEP 7: **Tie the third row.** Use a lark's head knot to attach the remaining 70˝ (1.8m) strand to the driftwood to the left of the center section. Using the second strand on the left as the leading strand, tie a clove hitch onto it with each strand to the right.

STEP 8: **Start tying off the end.** To tie off the leading strand and create an even finish, bring the leading strand up and over the driftwood from front to back. Feed the end through the loop that forms (it should be to the left of the loop on the driftwood).

STEP 9: **Finish tying off.** Now, bring the strand behind and over the driftwood from back to front. Feed the end through the loop that forms at the bottom of the driftwood. Pull tight. The finished knot will resemble a lark's head knot.

STEP 10: **Fill the empty space.** When finished, there may still be an empty space between the two lark's head knots on the right. Use a lark's head knot to tie the 60˝ (1.5m) strand onto the right side of the bottom semicircle to fill the space. Position the knot with the back side facing front to mimic a clove hitch.

STEP 11: **Start the next section.** Use lark's head knots to tie the 11½´ (3.5m) strands to the driftwood to the left of the center section. For this section, you will create a diamond pattern using clove hitches and berry knots (which are a series of square knots).

Beachy Wall Hanging, *continued*

STEP 12: Start the diamond. Using the fifth strand on the left as the leading strand, tie a clove hitch onto it with each of the four stands to the left.

STEP 13: Finish the top of the diamond. Using the fifth strand again, tie a clove hitch onto it with each of the three strands to the right.

STEP 14: Tie the square knots. Using the four center strands, tie three square knots.

STEP 15: Make a space. Make a space in the center of the design between the point of the diamond and the top of the first square knot.

STEP 16: Pull the center strands through. Bring the two center strands up and through the space you made in Step 15 from front to back.

STEP 17: Pull tight. Pull the center strands tight. This will roll up the series of square knots you made in Step 14, forming a round berry shape.

STEP 18: Tie a square knot. To hold the berry knot in place, tie a square knot with the four center strands.

STEP 19: Finish the diamond. Using the outer left strand as the leading strand, tie a clove hitch onto it with each of the three strands to the right. Repeat on the right, tying a clove hitch onto the outer right strand with each of the three strands to the left. Close the diamond with a fourth clove hitch.

STEP 20: Repeat. Repeat Steps 12–19 to make three more diamonds. When you are finished, the left section should have a total of four diamonds with berry knots in the center.

Beachy Wall Hanging, *continued*

STEP 21: **Shape the semicircle.**
Bring the ends of the left section up and over the driftwood to the right of the center section, forming a large semicircle.

STEP 22A and 22B: **Start tying off.**
Take the end of the left strand and bring it to the front (Photo A). Wrap it around itself and the strand to the right and bring it to the back (Photo B).

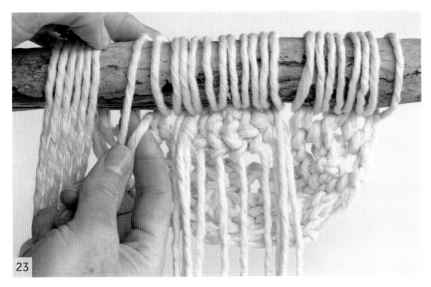

STEP 23: **Finish tying off.** Flip the driftwood over and tie the two strands together in a simple double knot at the back. When you look at the piece from the back, these will be the two right strands.

STEP 24A and 24B: **Repeat.** Repeat Steps 22–23 with the remaining strands, working in pairs.

STEP 25: **Attach the next set of cotton pieces.** Use lark's head knots to tie three 10′ (3m) pieces of cotton on each side of the center semicircle.

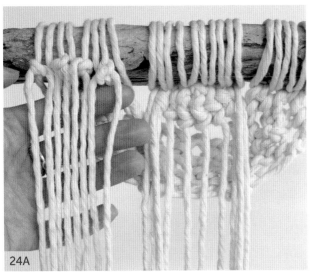

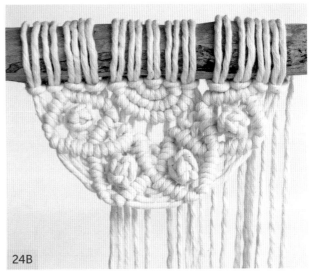

Beachy Wall Hanging, *continued*

STEP 26: Tie the diamonds. Follow the same technique used in Steps 12–19 to make three diamonds in each section. Instead of berry knots, use the center four strands to tie a single square knot in the center of each diamond.

STEP 27: Secure the semicircles. Bring the ends of each outside section up and over the driftwood, forming semicircles. Secure the ends of each semicircle following Steps 22–23.

26

27

STEP 28: Make the loops on the back. Turn the wall hanging around. Take the two outermost strands and tie them together to make one big loop. Now, tie three loops that mimic the semicircles on the front of the design. For example, take a strand near the left end of the driftwood. Shape it into a loop that matches the size of the left semicircle. Then, secure the end of the loop by tying it to the nearest strand at the back of the driftwood. Repeat with the remaining two semicircles. These layers do not need to be as neat as the front of the design.

STEP 29: Start adding the fringe. Use lark's head knots to attach the 44″ (1.1m) cotton pieces to the large loop at the back of the design. In my design, I used four pieces of recycled silk and twenty-four pieces of cotton.

28

29

Beachy Wall Hanging, *continued*

STEP 30: Trim. Now that the longest fringe pieces have been added, I like to trim them to shape the bottom of the wall hanging. You can save the trimmings for some of the short layers of fringe in the next steps. My design measures 28˝ (71cm) from the top of the driftwood to the bottom of the fringe in the center. I trimmed each side of the fringe to give the bottom edge a semicircular shape.

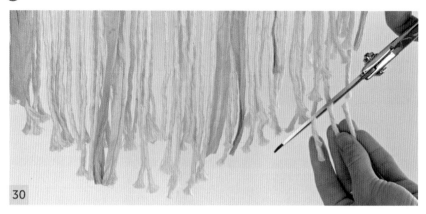

STEP 31: Finish adding the fringe. Use lark's head knots to attach the 25˝ (63.5cm) pieces of cotton to the center loop at the back of the design. Then, add eight 16˝ (40.5cm) pieces to each outside loop. Once you have added all the fringe pieces, push them through the large loop so they are on top of the long fringe when you view the design from the front.

STEP 32: Check your work. When you look at the wall hanging from the front, it should look something like this.

STEP 33: Add the short fringe pieces. Use lark's head knots to attach additional short fringe pieces to the semicircles, filling in any open spaces between the knots. This is a great way to use up any scraps you have from trimming the long fringe in Step 30. I added about eight 5" (13cm) fringe pieces to the center semicircle and four pieces to each of the outer semicircles.

STEP 34: Finish. Comb out the short pieces of fringe and trim them.

STEP 35: Embellish. You can leave your wall hanging as is or embellish it further. I glued a shell in the middle of the large semicircle and added five wooden beads to the bottom of the fringe. I also used some of the fringe pieces to create two braided layers.

Boho Style Inspiration

Décor Ideas to Complement Your Macramé Designs.

Love the laid-back look of boho décor and want to recreate it in your home? Here are some of my favorite items to pair with macramé projects to create a cozy, layered, and eclectic look.

Nubby textured pillows and houseplants make a perfect complement for the Beachy Wall Hanging.

Light-colored wood furniture and soft leather are beautiful textures to complement your macramé designs.

The boho bedroom is not complete without layers and layers of soft pillows and blankets. Add a hand-dyed textile and your favorite macramé piece to complete the look.

Nothing says boho like a good hat, and these straw ones serve double duty as wall décor. You can also mix wicker baskets and other woven items with your macramé to create a rustic look. Scour vintage stores and flea markets for one-of-a-kind finds.

Patterns

The Feather and Rainbow projects have handy patterns that you can use to cut out the felt backings. The feather pattern is also a helpful guide when you trim the edges to make the feather shape. In the case of the rainbows, the pattern will help you size each row and create the proper arch shape.

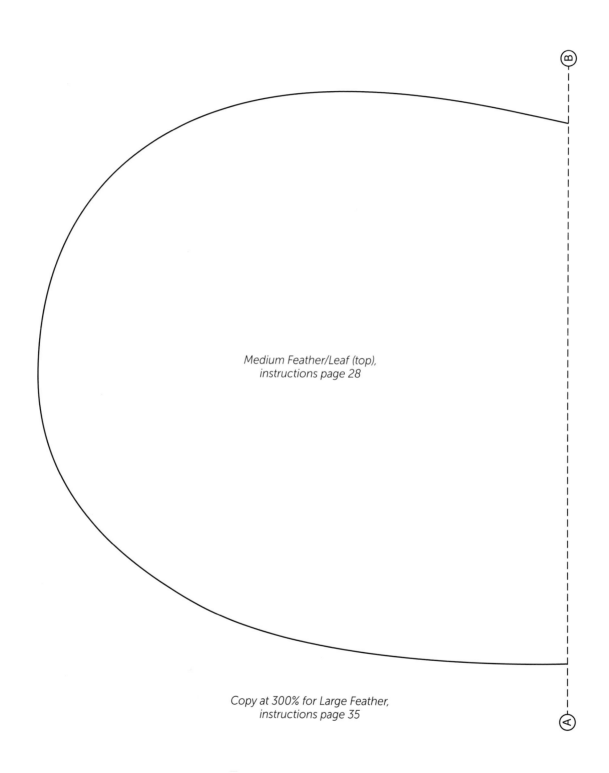

Ⓑ

*Medium Feather/Leaf (top),
instructions page 28*

*Copy at 300% for Large Feather,
instructions page 35*

Ⓐ

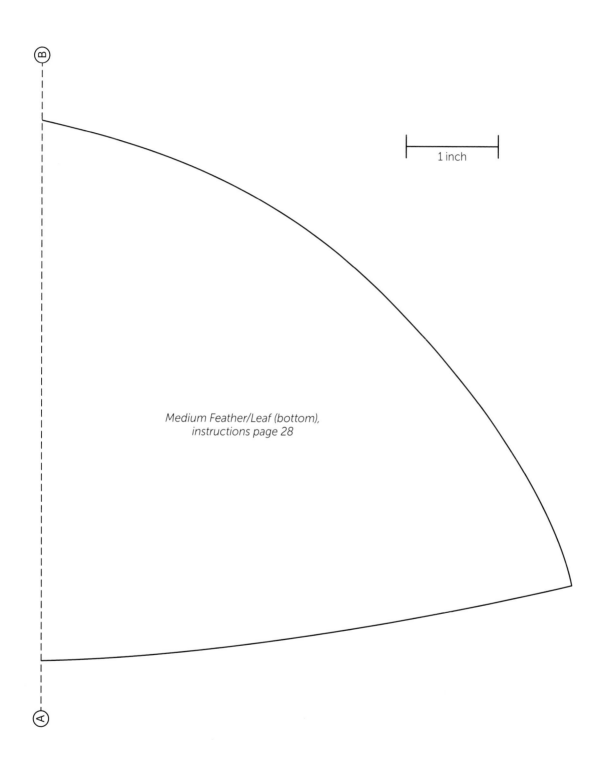

B

A

1 inch

Medium Feather/Leaf (bottom),
instructions page 28

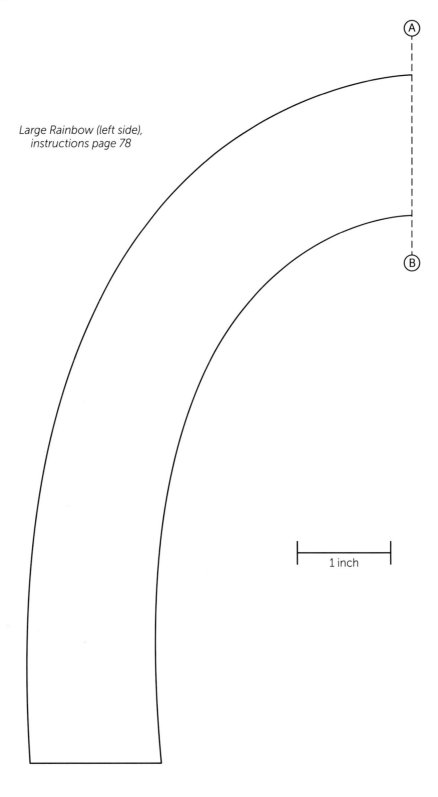

*Large Rainbow (left side),
instructions page 78*

Ⓐ

Ⓑ

1 inch

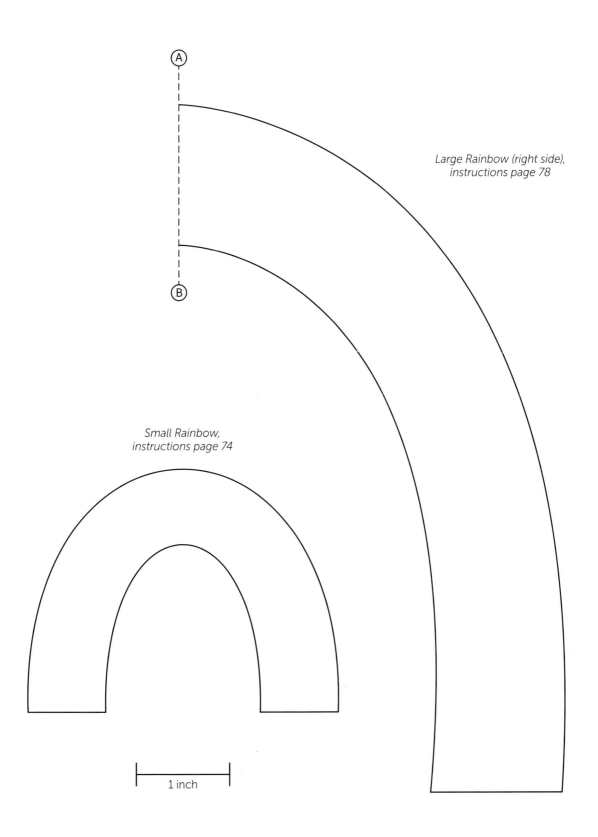

Large Rainbow (right side),
instructions page 78

Small Rainbow,
instructions page 74

1 inch

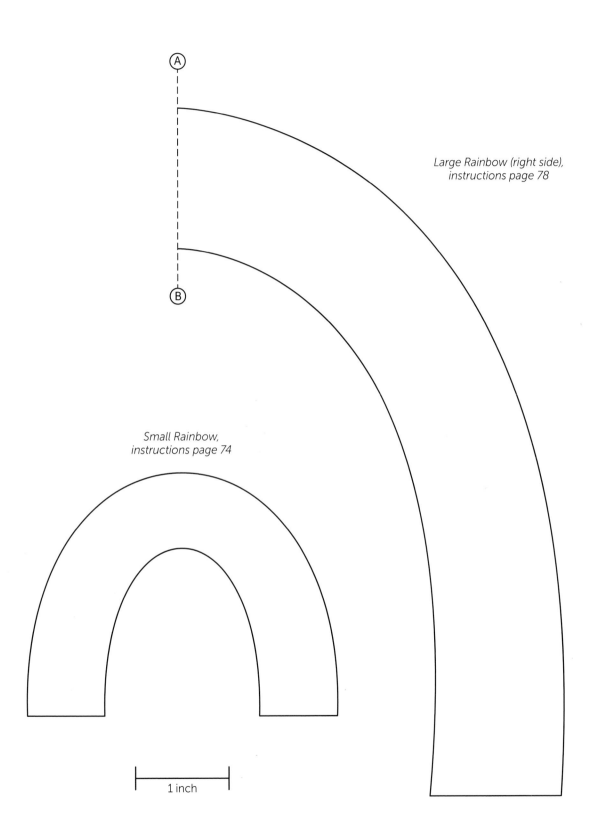

(A)

*Large Rainbow (right side),
instructions page 78*

(B)

*Small Rainbow,
instructions page 74*

127

Patterns

1 inch